**Volu**

Adress:

Name: **Email:**

Phone :   **Organisation :**

Date	Hours	Activity	Supervisor Sign

Notes ————————————————————
————————————————————

Volunteer Tracker

Adress:

Name: **Email:**

Phone :   **Organisation :**

Date	Hours	Activity	Supervisor Sign

Notes ——————————————————
————————————————————————

Volunteer Tracker

Adress:			
Name:		Email:	
Phone :		Organisation :	

Date	Hours	Activity	Supervisor Sign

Notes ——————————————————
————————————————————————

Volunteer Tracker

Adress:	
Name:	Email:
Phone :	Organisation :

Date	Hours	Activity	Supervisor Sign

Notes ————————————————

Volunteer Tracker

Adress:

Name: Email:

Phone :   Organisation :

Date	Hours	Activity	Supervisor Sign

Notes ——————————————————
————————————————————————

Volunteer Tracker

Adress:

Name: Email:

Phone :   Organisation :

Date	Hours	Activity	Supervisor Sign

Notes ————————————————
————————————————

Volunteer Tracker

Adress:			
Name:		Email:	
Phone :		Organisation :	

Date	Hours	Activity	Supervisor Sign

Notes _____
_____

Volunteer Tracker

Adress:	
Name:	Email:
Phone :	Organisation :

Date	Hours	Activity	Supervisor Sign

Notes ————————————————

Volunteer Tracker

Adress:			
Name:		Email:	
Phone :		Organisation :	

Date	Hours	Activity	Supervisor Sign

Notes _____
_____

Volunteer Tracker

Adress:			
Name:		Email:	
Phone :		Organisation :	

Date	Hours	Activity	Supervisor Sign

Notes

Volunteer Tracker

Adress:			
Name:		Email:	
Phone :		Organisation :	

Date	Hours	Activity	Supervisor Sign

Notes ——————————————————
————————————————————

Volunteer Tracker

Adress:	
Name:	Email:
Phone :	Organisation :

Date	Hours	Activity	Supervisor Sign

Notes _____

_____

Volunteer Tracker

Adress:		
Name:	Email:	
Phone :	Organisation :	

Date	Hours	Activity	Supervisor Sign

Notes _____
_____

Volunteer Tracker

Adress:			
Name:		Email:	
Phone :		Organisation :	

Date	Hours	Activity	Supervisor Sign

Notes —————————————————

Volunteer Tracker

Adress:	
Name:	Email:
Phone :	Organisation :

Date	Hours	Activity	Supervisor Sign

Notes ――――――――――――――――――
―――――――――――――――――――――

Volunteer Tracker

Adress:			
Name:		Email:	
Phone :		Organisation :	

Date	Hours	Activity	Supervisor Sign

Notes ——————————————————————
————————————————————————

Volunteer Tracker

Adress:

Name: Email:

Phone :   Organisation :

Date	Hours	Activity	Supervisor Sign

Notes _____

_____

Volunteer Tracker

Adress:			
Name:		Email:	
Phone :		Organisation :	

Date	Hours	Activity	Supervisor Sign

Notes ——————————————————
———————————————————————

Volunteer Tracker

Adress:			
Name:		Email:	
Phone :		Organisation :	

Date	Hours	Activity	Supervisor Sign

Notes _____

_____

Volunteer Tracker

Adress:	
Name:	Email:
Phone :	Organisation :

Date	Hours	Activity	Supervisor Sign

Notes _____
_____

Volunteer Tracker

Adress:			
Name:		Email:	
Phone :		Organisation :	

Date	Hours	Activity	Supervisor Sign

Notes ——————————————————

————————————————————

Volunteer Tracker

Adress:			
Name:		Email:	
Phone :		Organisation :	

Date	Hours	Activity	Supervisor Sign

Notes ———————————————
————————————————————

Volunteer Tracker

Adress:

Name: Email:

Phone :   Organisation :

Date	Hours	Activity	Supervisor Sign

Notes —————————————————————
————————————————————————

Volunteer Tracker

Adress:			
Name:		Email:	
Phone :		Organisation :	

Date	Hours	Activity	Supervisor Sign

Notes ————————————

Volunteer Tracker

Adress:

Name: Email:

Phone :   Organisation :

Date	Hours	Activity	Supervisor Sign

Notes —————————————————
—————————————————

Volunteer Tracker

Adress:	
Name:	Email:
Phone :	Organisation :

Date	Hours	Activity	Supervisor Sign

Notes

Volunteer Tracker

Adress:		
Name:	Email:	
Phone :	Organisation :	

Date	Hours	Activity	Supervisor Sign

Notes ——————————————————
———————————————————————

Volunteer Tracker

Adress:			
Name:		Email:	
Phone :		Organisation :	

Date	Hours	Activity	Supervisor Sign

Notes _____
_____

Volunteer Tracker

Adress:

Name: Email:

Phone :   Organisation :

Date	Hours	Activity	Supervisor Sign

Notes —————————————————

————————————————————

Volunteer Tracker

Adress:	
Name:	Email:
Phone :	Organisation :

Date	Hours	Activity	Supervisor Sign

Notes _____
_____

Volunteer Tracker

Adress:			
Name:		Email:	
Phone :		Organisation :	

Date	Hours	Activity	Supervisor Sign

Notes

Volunteer Tracker

Adress:	
Name:	Email:
Phone :	Organisation :

Date	Hours	Activity	Supervisor Sign

Notes _____

_____

Volunteer Tracker

Adress:

Name: Email:

Phone :   Organisation :

Date	Hours	Activity	Supervisor Sign

Notes ————————————————

————————————————

Volunteer Tracker

Adress:			
Name:		Email:	
Phone :		Organisation :	

Date	Hours	Activity	Supervisor Sign

Notes —————————————————
————————————————————

Volunteer Tracker

Adress:			
Name:		Email:	
Phone :		Organisation :	

Date	Hours	Activity	Supervisor Sign

Notes _____
_____

Volunteer Tracker

Adress:			
Name:		Email:	
Phone :		Organisation :	

Date	Hours	Activity	Supervisor Sign

Notes ————————————————————
————————————————————————

Volunteer Tracker

Adress:

Name: Email:

Phone :   Organisation :

Date	Hours	Activity	Supervisor Sign

Notes ————————————————————————

————————————————————————

Volunteer Tracker

Adress:			
Name:		Email:	
Phone :		Organisation :	

Date	Hours	Activity	Supervisor Sign

Notes _____

_____

Volunteer Tracker

Adress:			
Name:		Email:	
Phone :		Organisation :	

Date	Hours	Activity	Supervisor Sign

Notes ——————————————————
————————————————————

Volunteer Tracker

Adress:	
Name:	Email:
Phone :	Organisation :

Date	Hours	Activity	Supervisor Sign

Notes _____
_____

Volunteer Tracker

Adress:			
Name:		Email:	
Phone :		Organisation :	

Date	Hours	Activity	Supervisor Sign

Notes ――――――――――――――――――――

――――――――――――――――――――

Volunteer Tracker

Adress:			
Name:		Email:	
Phone :		Organisation :	

Date	Hours	Activity	Supervisor Sign

Notes ———————————————————
———————————————————————

Volunteer Tracker

Adress:

Name: Email:

Phone :   Organisation :

Date	Hours	Activity	Supervisor Sign

Notes ————————————————————
————————————————————

Volunteer Tracker

Adress:			
Name:		Email:	
Phone :		Organisation :	

Date	Hours	Activity	Supervisor Sign

Notes ————————————————
————————————————————

Volunteer Tracker

Adress:	
Name:	Email:
Phone :	Organisation :

Date	Hours	Activity	Supervisor Sign

Notes ————————————————
————————————————

Volunteer Tracker

Adress:			
Name:		Email:	
Phone :		Organisation :	

Date	Hours	Activity	Supervisor Sign

Notes —————————————————————

Volunteer Tracker

Adress:

Name: **Email:**

Phone : **Organisation :**

Date	Hours	Activity	Supervisor Sign

Notes ———————————————————

—————————————————————

Volunteer Tracker

Adress:	
Name:	Email:
Phone :	Organisation :

Date	Hours	Activity	Supervisor Sign

Notes ——————————————————

Volunteer Tracker

Adress:	
Name:	Email:
Phone :	Organisation :

Date	Hours	Activity	Supervisor Sign

Notes ——————————————————

————————————————————————

Volunteer Tracker

Adress:

Name: **Email:**

Phone :   **Organisation :**

Date	Hours	Activity	Supervisor Sign

Notes ⸺⸺⸺⸺⸺⸺⸺⸺⸺⸺⸺

Volunteer Tracker

Adress:	
Name:	Email:
Phone :	Organisation :

Date	Hours	Activity	Supervisor Sign

Notes ——————————————————————

————————————————————————

Volunteer Tracker

Adress:			
Name:		Email:	
Phone :		Organisation :	

Date	Hours	Activity	Supervisor Sign

Notes —————————————————
—————————————————

Volunteer Tracker

Adress:

Name: Email:

Phone :   Organisation :

Date	Hours	Activity	Supervisor Sign

Notes ————————————————
————————————————

Volunteer Tracker

Adress:			
Name:		Email:	
Phone :		Organisation :	

Date	Hours	Activity	Supervisor Sign

Notes ——————————————————————
——————————————————————

Volunteer Tracker

Adress:			
Name:		Email:	
Phone :		Organisation :	

Date	Hours	Activity	Supervisor Sign

Notes _____

_____

Volunteer Tracker

Adress:

Name: Email:

Phone :   Organisation :

Date	Hours	Activity	Supervisor Sign

Notes ———————————————————

————————————————————————

Volunteer Tracker

Adress:

Name: Email:

Phone :   Organisation :

Date	Hours	Activity	Supervisor Sign

Notes ———————————————
———————————————

Volunteer Tracker

Adress:			
Name:		Email:	
Phone :		Organisation :	

Date	Hours	Activity	Supervisor Sign

Notes —————————————————
—————————————————

Volunteer Tracker

Adress:			
Name:		Email:	
Phone :		Organisation :	

Date	Hours	Activity	Supervisor Sign

Notes ——————————————————
———————————————————

Volunteer Tracker

Adress:	
Name:	Email:
Phone :	Organisation :

Date	Hours	Activity	Supervisor Sign

Notes —————————————
—————————————

Volunteer Tracker

Adress:

Name: Email:

Phone :   Organisation :

Date	Hours	Activity	Supervisor Sign

Notes ——————————————————————
——————————————————————

Volunteer Tracker

Adress:	
Name:	Email:
Phone :	Organisation :

Date	Hours	Activity	Supervisor Sign

Notes ————————————————
————————————————

Volunteer Tracker

Adress:		
Name:	Email:	
Phone :	Organisation :	

Date	Hours	Activity	Supervisor Sign

Notes —————————————————————

Volunteer Tracker

Adress:

Name: Email:

Phone :   Organisation :

Date	Hours	Activity	Supervisor Sign

Notes ———————————————————————

Volunteer Tracker

Adress:

Name: Email:

Phone :   Organisation :

Date	Hours	Activity	Supervisor Sign

Notes _____

_____

Volunteer Tracker

Adress:			
Name:		Email:	
Phone :		Organisation :	

Date	Hours	Activity	Supervisor Sign

Notes ——————————————————
————————————————————————

Volunteer Tracker

Adress:			
Name:		Email:	
Phone :		Organisation :	

Date	Hours	Activity	Supervisor Sign

Notes ―――――――――――――――――――――
―――――――――――――――――――――

Volunteer Tracker

Adress:			
Name:		Email:	
Phone :		Organisation :	

Date	Hours	Activity	Supervisor Sign

Notes ⎯⎯⎯⎯⎯⎯⎯⎯⎯⎯⎯⎯⎯⎯⎯⎯
⎯⎯⎯⎯⎯⎯⎯⎯⎯⎯⎯⎯⎯⎯⎯⎯⎯⎯⎯⎯

Volunteer Tracker

Adress:			
Name:		Email:	
Phone :		Organisation :	

Date	Hours	Activity	Supervisor Sign

Notes —————————————————————

Volunteer Tracker

Adress:			
Name:		Email:	
Phone :		Organisation :	

Date	Hours	Activity	Supervisor Sign

Notes ——————————————————
————————————————————

Volunteer Tracker

Adress:		
Name:	Email:	
Phone :	Organisation :	

Date	Hours	Activity	Supervisor Sign

Notes ————————————————————
————————————————————————

Volunteer Tracker

Adress:			
Name:		Email:	
Phone :		Organisation :	

Date	Hours	Activity	Supervisor Sign

Notes ———————————————

———————————————

Volunteer Tracker

Adress:			
Name:		Email:	
Phone :		Organisation :	

Date	Hours	Activity	Supervisor Sign

Notes —————————————————
———————————————————

Volunteer Tracker

Adress:	
Name:	Email:
Phone :	Organisation :

Date	Hours	Activity	Supervisor Sign

Notes —————————————————
——————————————————————

Volunteer Tracker

Adress:		
Name:	Email:	
Phone :	Organisation :	

Date	Hours	Activity	Supervisor Sign

Notes ——————————————
————————————————

Volunteer Tracker

Adress:			
Name:		Email:	
Phone :		Organisation :	

Date	Hours	Activity	Supervisor Sign

Notes ——————————————————
——————————————————

Volunteer Tracker

Adress:

Name: Email:

Phone :   Organisation :

Date	Hours	Activity	Supervisor Sign

Notes ————————————————
————————————————

Volunteer Tracker

Adress:	
Name:	Email:
Phone :	Organisation :

Date	Hours	Activity	Supervisor Sign

Notes —————————————
—————————————

Volunteer Tracker

Adress:

Name: Email:

Phone :   Organisation :

Date	Hours	Activity	Supervisor Sign

Notes _____

_____

Volunteer Tracker

Adress:			
Name:		Email:	
Phone :		Organisation :	

Date	Hours	Activity	Supervisor Sign

Notes ——————————————————
————————————————————————

Volunteer Tracker

Adress:			
Name:		Email:	
Phone :		Organisation :	

Date	Hours	Activity	Supervisor Sign

Notes _____

_____

Volunteer Tracker

Adress:			
Name:		Email:	
Phone :		Organisation :	

Date	Hours	Activity	Supervisor Sign

Notes ——————————————————
——————————————————

Volunteer Tracker

Adress:			
Name:		Email:	
Phone :		Organisation :	

Date	Hours	Activity	Supervisor Sign

Notes ——————————————————
——————————————————

Volunteer Tracker

Adress:	
Name:	Email:
Phone :	Organisation :

Date	Hours	Activity	Supervisor Sign

Notes —————————————————
—————————————————

Volunteer Tracker

Adress:

Name: Email:

Phone :   Organisation :

Date	Hours	Activity	Supervisor Sign

Notes ——————————————————
————————————————————

Volunteer Tracker

Adress:			
Name:		Email:	
Phone :		Organisation :	

Date	Hours	Activity	Supervisor Sign

Notes _____

_____

Volunteer Tracker

Adress:			
Name:		Email:	
Phone :		Organisation :	

Date	Hours	Activity	Supervisor Sign

Notes _____
_____

Volunteer Tracker

Adress:			
Name:		Email:	
Phone :		Organisation :	

Date	Hours	Activity	Supervisor Sign

Notes ——————————————————

Volunteer Tracker

Adress:

Name: Email:

Phone :   Organisation :

Date	Hours	Activity	Supervisor Sign

Notes ————————————————————

————————————————————————

Volunteer Tracker

Adress:		
Name:	Email:	
Phone :	Organisation :	

Date	Hours	Activity	Supervisor Sign

Notes ———————————————————

——————————————————————

Volunteering Tracker

Adress:

Name: **Email:**

Phone :   **Organisation :**

Date	Hours	Activity	Supervisor Sign

Notes ——————————————————————
——————————————————————————————

Volunteer Tracker

Adress:

Name: Email:

Phone :   Organisation :

Date	Hours	Activity	Supervisor Sign

Notes —————————————————
—————————————————————————

Volunteer Tracker

Adress:			
Name:		Email:	
Phone :		Organisation :	

Date	Hours	Activity	Supervisor Sign

Notes —————————————————————————
————————————————————————————

Volunteer Tracker

Adress:	
Name:	Email:
Phone :	Organisation :

Date	Hours	Activity	Supervisor Sign

Notes —————————————————————

Volunteer Tracker

Adress:

Name: Email:

Phone :   Organisation :

Date	Hours	Activity	Supervisor Sign

Notes ⎯⎯⎯⎯⎯⎯⎯⎯⎯⎯⎯⎯⎯⎯⎯⎯⎯⎯⎯⎯
⎯⎯⎯⎯⎯⎯⎯⎯⎯⎯⎯⎯⎯⎯⎯⎯⎯⎯⎯⎯⎯⎯⎯⎯

Volunteer Tracker

Adress:			
Name:		Email:	
Phone :		Organisation :	

Date	Hours	Activity	Supervisor Sign

Notes _____

_____

Volunteer Tracker

Adress:			
Name:		Email:	
Phone :		Organisation :	

Date	Hours	Activity	Supervisor Sign

Notes _____

_____

Volunteer Tracker

Adress:	
Name:	Email:
Phone :	Organisation :

Date	Hours	Activity	Supervisor Sign

Notes ——————————————
——————————————

Volunteer Tracker

Adress:

Name: Email:

Phone :   Organisation :

Date	Hours	Activity	Supervisor Sign

Notes _____

_____

Volunteer Tracker

Adress:			
Name:		Email:	
Phone :		Organisation :	

Date	Hours	Activity	Supervisor Sign

Notes _____

_____

Volunteer Tracker

Adress:	
Name:	Email:
Phone :	Organisation :

Date	Hours	Activity	Supervisor Sign

Notes —————————————————————

Volunteer Tracker

Adress:	
Name:	Email:
Phone :	Organisation :

Date	Hours	Activity	Supervisor Sign

Notes

Volunteer Tracker

Adress:	
Name:	Email:
Phone :	Organisation :

Date	Hours	Activity	Supervisor Sign

Notes ——————————————————
——————————————————————

Volunteer Tracker

Adress:		
Name:	Email:	
Phone :	Organisation :	

Date	Hours	Activity	Supervisor Sign

Notes ―――――――――――――
―――――――――――――

Volunteer Tracker

Adress:	
Name:	Email:
Phone :	Organisation :

Date	Hours	Activity	Supervisor Sign

Notes —————————————————————
—————————————————————

Volunteer Tracker

Adress:

Name: Email:

Phone :   Organisation :

Date	Hours	Activity	Supervisor Sign

Notes ————————————————
————————————————————

Volunteer Tracker

Adress:			
Name:		Email:	
Phone :		Organisation :	

Date	Hours	Activity	Supervisor Sign

Notes ——————————————————————
——————————————————————

Volunteer Tracker

Adress:		
Name:	Email:	
Phone :	Organisation :	

Date	Hours	Activity	Supervisor Sign

Notes ——————————————————————
——————————————————————

Volunteer Tracker

Adress:

Name: Email:

Phone :   Organisation :

Date	Hours	Activity	Supervisor Sign

Notes ————————————————
————————————————————

Volunteer Tracker

Adress:	
Name:	Email:
Phone :	Organisation :

Date	Hours	Activity	Supervisor Sign

Notes —————————————————
—————————————————

Volunteer Tracker

Adress:			
Name:		Email:	
Phone :		Organisation :	

Date	Hours	Activity	Supervisor Sign

Notes ————————————————
————————————————

Volunteer Tracker

Adress:			
Name:		Email:	
Phone :		Organisation :	

Date	Hours	Activity	Supervisor Sign

Notes

Volunteer Tracker

Adress:

Name: Email:

Phone :   Organisation :

Date	Hours	Activity	Supervisor Sign

Notes

Volunteer Tracker

Adress:

Name: **Email:**

Phone :   **Organisation :**

Date	Hours	Activity	Supervisor Sign

Notes ―――――――――――――――――――――――
―――――――――――――――――――――――

Volunteer Tracker

Adress:

Name: Email:

Phone :   Organisation :

Date	Hours	Activity	Supervisor Sign

Notes _____

_____

Volunteer Tracker

Adress:		
Name:	Email:	
Phone :	Organisation :	

Date	Hours	Activity	Supervisor Sign

Notes ————————————————————
————————————————————

Volunteer Tracker

Adress:			
Name:		Email:	
Phone :		Organisation :	

Date	Hours	Activity	Supervisor Sign

Notes —————————————————
————————————————————

Volunteer Tracker

Adress:			
Name:		Email:	
Phone :		Organisation :	

Date	Hours	Activity	Supervisor Sign

Notes —————————————————————
————————————————————

Volunteer Tracker

Adress:

Name: Email:

Phone :   Organisation :

Date	Hours	Activity	Supervisor Sign

Notes —————————————————————

————————————————————————

Volunteer Tracker

Adress:	
Name:	Email:
Phone :	Organisation :

Date	Hours	Activity	Supervisor Sign

Notes ───────────────────────
_____

24930787R00069